SR

Books are to be returned on or before
the last date below.

EXTREME SPORT

WATER SPORTS

Jim Gigliotti

www.raintreepublishers.co.uk
Visit our website to find out more information about Raintree books.

To order:
☎ Phone 0845 6044371
🖷 Fax +44 (0) 1865 312263
✉ Email myorders@raintreepublishers.co.uk

Customers from outside the UK please telephone +44 1865 312262

Raintree is an imprint of Capstone Global Library Limited, a company incorporated in England and Wales having its registered office at 7 Pilgrim Street, London, EC4V 6LB – Registered company number: 6695582

Edited by Rebecca Rissman, Dan Nunn, and Catherine Veitch
Designed by Joanna Hinton Malivoire
Picture research by Ruth Blair
Originated by Capstone Global Library
Printed and bound in China by CTPS

ISBN 978 1 406 22694 2
15 14 13 12 11
10 9 8 7 6 5 4 3 2 1

British Library Cataloguing in Publication Data
Gigliotti, Jim
Water sports. – (Extreme sport)
797-dc22
A full catalogue record for this book is available from the British Library.

Acknowledgements
We would like to thank the following for permission to reproduce photographs: Corbis pp. 4 (© Patrick B. Kraemer/epa), 6 (© Fei Maohua/xh/Xinhua Press), 9 (© Robert Benson/Aurora Photos), 17 (© Joseba Etxaburu/Reuters), 23 (© Elizabeth Kreutz/NewSport), 29 (© Serge Kozak); Getty Images p. 16 (AFP); Shutterstock pp. 5 (© Junial Enterprises), 7 (© robcocquyt), 8 (© muzsy), 10 (© Paul Binet), 11 (© Neale Cousland), 12 (© Dejan Lazarevic), 13 (© VitCOM Photo), 14 (© Bluerain), 15 (© Ventura), 18 (© Pierre-Yves Babelon), 19 (© Pierre-Yves Babelon), 20 (© jarvis gray), 21 (© cassiede alain), 22 (© alysta), 24 (© Poznyakov), 25 (© VanHart), 26 (© Lee Torrens), 27 (© bikeriderlondon), 28 (© Alexander Ishchenko).

Cover photograph of a woman on a jet ski reproduced with permission of Corbis (© Richard Hamilton Smith).

Every effort has been made to contact copyright holders of material reproduced in this book. Any omissions will be rectified in subsequent printings if notice is given to the publisher.

Some words are shown in bold, **like this**. You can find out what they mean by looking in the glossary.

Contents

Water sport

Swimming is a lot of fun. It's great exercise, too. Let's look at some other sports that also are a lot of fun and great exercise in – or on – the water!

STAY SAFE!

The sports you'll read about in this book are all done by experienced sportspeople. To learn how to stay safe in the water, see page 24.

Diving

In diving competitions, athletes dive from boards up to 10 metres in the air. That's taller than a two-storey house! A more extreme form of diving is cliff diving. Divers leap from cliffs that are as high above the water as an eight-storey building.

DID YOU KNOW?

Cliff diving is so dangerous that it is also called tombstoning. NEVER do this yourself.

Harder than it looks

Water polo looks like a lot of fun! Players swim in the water and try to throw a ball into a net to score goals. Water polo is hard work! Swimmers need strong legs to **tread water**. They also need strong arms to keep **opponents** away from the ball.

Skiing ... on water!

Water skiing looks a lot like snow skiing – except it's on water! Water skiers are pulled along by a motorboat. Sometimes, water skiers do tricks or jumps. Some water skiers use only one ski! This is called slalom skiing.

Jet skiing

Jet skiers race along the water as if on a motorcycle without wheels. A jet ski is a personal watercraft, or PWC. It seats one or two people, and it has a powerful motor. Some jet skiers like to compete against others in **freestyle** events or races.

WOW!

Some athletes go over rapids in small **kayaks**. Paddle hard!

Surf's up!

Surfing was one of the original extreme sports. People in the South Pacific have surfed for hundreds of years. Surfers stand on a board and ride the surface of the water.

DID YOU KNOW?

Surfing's got a language of its own:
- *catch a wave* – begin a ride
- *hang ten* – hanging all 10 toes over the nose of a surfboard
- *ride the tube* – surf the space under a curling wave.

A different type of surfing

Imagine combining surfing and sailing. What do you have? Windsurfing! Windsurfers stand on a board like a surfboard. They hold on to a sail attached to the board.

WOW!

A good windsurfer can move the sail to pick up speed and do tricks.

Bodyboarding

Bodyboarders use a small board. Sometimes they stand, or ride with one knee on the board. Most of the time, though, they lie on their stomachs. Bodyboarders do stunts. They leap off the **crest** of a wave and spin through the air before splashing back down!

Extreme extreme sports

Would you believe that these sports aren't extreme enough for some athletes? They've made up sports that are even more extreme! Wakeboarders are pulled behind a motorboat, just like water skiers. But wakeboarders stand on a wider board and do tricks high in the air!

Barefoot skiing is water skiing
without the skis!

Be safe!

For all water sports the number one rule is to be safe. The first step in water safety is to learn to swim well. Take lessons from a **qualified** instructor. Always swim with your parents or a lifeguard watching. Use the buddy system, too, and swim with a friend.

STAY SAFE!
Swim in safe, guarded areas. If you dive, dive only where it is allowed.

Staying healthy

Athletes have to be physically fit whatever the water sport. **Agility** and **endurance** are important for athletes in water sports. To build those areas, proper exercise and **nutrition** is the first step. Make it your first step, too!

Get fit!

Do you want to get into water sport? Try to do at least 60 to 90 minutes of exercise each day. You could ride your bike or climb on playground **equipment**. Even if you don't get involved in water sport, you'll feel great!

Glossary

agility ability to move quickly and easily

crest foamy top of a wave

endurance able to last for a long time, for example, while playing sport

equipment tools or clothing that you need for a particular activity

freestyle event in which competitors can use any style they wish

hurtle move quickly and with great force

kayak type of canoe for one person

nutrition food that keeps you healthy

opponent someone who is against you in a competition

qualified trained and able to do a job

tread water swimming to keep upright and with the head above water

Find out more

Books

101 Youth Fitness Drills Age 7–11, John Shepherd and Mike Antoniades (A & C Black, 2010)

Starting Sport: Swimming, Rebecca Hunter (Franklin Watts, 2008)

To the Limit: Surfing, Paul Mason (Wayland, 2008)

World Sports Guide: Windsurfing, Paul Mason (A & C Black, 2010)

Websites

www.bbc.co.uk/northernireland/schools/4_11/uptoyou/
This website has lots of information about healthy eating and exercise. Why not get fit and enjoy some extreme sports?

www.britishwaterski.org.uk/UKSki/DesktopDefault.aspx?tabid=221
This website tells you all about the 'Cutting Edge' youth scheme from British Water Ski and Wakeboard. You can download posters, stretch routines, and information about the different types of water sport.

Index